M000202441

The Edge of the Playground

Mary Lynn Ackerman Willis &

Mikhaela Ackerman

Copyright © 2019 by Mary Lynn Ackerman Willis & Mikhaela
Ackerman. All rights reserved.

All rights reserved. No part of this publication may be reproduced,
distributed, or transmitted in any form or by any means, including
photocopying, recording, or other electronic or mechanical
methods, without the prior written permission of the publisher,
except in the case of brief quotations embodied in critical reviews
and certain other noncommercial uses permitted by copyright
law.

This book is a memoir. It reflects the author's present recollections
of experiences over time. Some names and characteristics
have been changed to protect privacy, some events have been
compressed, and some dialogue has been recreated.

ISBN: 978-0-578-56430-2 (Paperback)

Front cover image and design by Amira Shagaga.

Edge of the Playground, LLC.

First printing edition 2019.

www.edgeoftheplayground.com

Dedicated in loving memory of Marian James Ackerman,
Baba extraordinaire.

For carrying our family.

For her unwavering spirit and grace under pressure, always.

"The ability to tie your shoes does not determine your success."

1

Mikhaela

Recess. In one word: chaotic. Something I do not look forward to. I hear the teacher say it is time for recess. The other children become loud and rambunctious. They quickly flee the classroom to the outdoors. Faster than I can even realize what is happening.

I slowly walk outside to the playground. I am immediately met with a storming sea of bright lights, colors so vibrant I can barely open my eyes, and the loud voices of children at play. I am drowning. I have capsized. Carried out to sea with no escape. I see no faces, the only thing before me is painfully vibrant color with no place to rest my eyes. Like a bright, glaring light turned on too soon after being in complete darkness. Even the faintest light feels as if I am staring directly into the sun. Smells overwhelm me. The sounds are so loud I can distinguish no specific noise or words. Hearing each sound with equal intensity and no ability to filter out background noise. Jolting sounds that do not allow me to process what is being spoken. Constant input.

I need to find refuge. I cannot stay in this place.

I walk until the sounds slowly begin to fade away and the colors and brightness are not as enveloping. I walk and walk until finally I find peace. The place I have found is perfect for me. It is calm, there is not a lot going on. There are even straight lines made out of wood that I can walk and line things up on. I am close to the trees and feel relaxed. I have found my own little sanctuary amidst this sensory onslaught. Here, I am safe.

This place I have found is the edge of the playground.

I see no reason to leave. I am not lonely here. I am content. I am able to enter a meditative state by walking the edge. I do not want other children to approach me. They are too loud. What games could they possibly play more fun than my own imagination? I entertain myself very well. I crave this solitude. Befriending them is too difficult and interpreting social behavior is exhausting.

"You are all alone."

I look up. A girl. She has come to the edge of the playground.

Why has she come here? I think.

I do not need her here. I did not even ask her to come over. I am happy where I am. I look her way, and I am confused by this behavior.

"Let's be friends! Come with me I'll introduce you to the others and you can play with us."

Once again, I am confused. Why do these others desire my company? Why do they choose to be in this sensory storm day in and day out? I do not need friends; I am happy in my own world and my own space. The rest of the playground is overwhelming.

But deep down I wonder what friendship has to offer. Why people feel such a joy when being together. I find myself considering this invitation. Entering their world comes with a price. I know that. The price is learning a language that will always be foreign to me. Social and nonverbal language I don't easily understand…a language I never fully grasp. There's an eternal guessing game, along with the sensory storm I cannot filter. Being part of their world would not be simple for me. But this girl is inviting me. Maybe I will join. After all, I can always return to this place.

As I tentatively follow her from the edge of the playground into the storm, a single thought runs through my mind. *Is it worth it?*

2

Mary Lynn

Mikhaela's journey began in the same way it does for all of us, safely tucked in her mother's womb. I felt wonderful during this time. I was invigorated and had no complications through the pregnancy. Mikhaela was definitely a wanted and loved child even before she arrived. It would not be until years later that this glorious time would come into question. As if on cue, and after 33 hours of labor, Mikhaela made her entrance on October 29th, 1991. Children rarely arrive on their due date. It was to be a sign of the need for predictability that was to follow.

The first ten days were uneventful. In fact, Mikhaela's grandfather remarked that she seemed far away. It was almost as if she wasn't completely in this world. She was unusually quiet. She had a certain distance in her eyes. This observation would also turn out to be prophetic. At about ten days old, Mikhaela burst forth. She was positively inconsolable. Repeated trips to the pediatrician yielded no answers. As the frustration mounted, it was decided by the doctor that I was simply overwhelmed with a first-time baby and that it was nothing more than colic. Feeding had been an issue since birth. She had difficulty latching on, and she tired easily. I would later discover that this low muscle tone and poor coordination were hallmarks of things to come. Mikhaela had difficulty eating and sleeping. She would only sleep in a snuggly pack facing outward. The moment she was laid in her bed, she began to wail. I noticed that if I kept my hand on her back, she would continue sleeping. This was the beginning of gravitational insecurity. I was diligent. Black sheets went up on the windows to block out all light. Mikhaela continued to wake every hour or so until the age of two and a half. Despite the challenges, I remained completely in awe of my new daughter. Through the tears, I have always felt blessed.

The first year of the journey was difficult because everything bothered baby Mikhaela. Light, sound, and touch were the biggest offenders. As a result, the baby remained distant, unable to learn from the environment around her. I tried desperately to engage her, but Mikhaela preferred her solitary world. Inanimate objects fascinated her. One in particular emerged as a favorite, and it was a lamb named Baa. Later, after diagnosis, this comfort would receive a name. It is called stimming. This is the way that autistic people regulate themselves, through movement, sound, or other behaviors. In Mikhaela's case, through twiddling Baa's ears. It was soon understood by all who entered Mikhaela's world, that Baa was essential to daily living. During that first part of the journey, although distant and easily overwhelmed, Mikhaela seemed happy in her own home. As long as she had Baa close by, life was good.

3

MIKHAELA

Stimming is how I remain calm in this over-whelming world. A world that is not made for neurotypes like mine. Everything is fast paced, bright, loud, and intense sensory stimulation. Our society thrives on this kind of environment. I flounder in it.

Have you ever watched something very satisfying to you? Like soap being carved or listening to the sound of rain. Just as these things calm you, stimming calms me. It has the ability to take me into a solitary, meditative world where I can reset and clear my mind. It helps me regulate my emotions.

Leaving the edge of the playground was not easy. I immediately realized the extent of the sacrifice I had made. I also knew that if I wanted to be independent in this world, there was no going back. No matter how much I might want to. In order to survive here, I need to stim. I need to find other escapes like the edge of the playground in my daily life. A quiet bathroom or an empty hallway work very well. Somewhere I can reset when it begins to feel overwhelming. A respite.

I never really noticed how different I was from other children. Most bullying, especially from girls, was nonverbal so I did not pick up on it. I can't even say I was bullied because of autism. But I was bullied because of my autistic traits (when kids saw me stimming or when I mirrored others to learn social behavior). Kids hate nothing more than people copying them. But copying and mimicking was my only way of being a part of their world. I had no way of understanding the world without doing this. This behavior is not a recipe for fast friends.

I wish I could tell you that I was a happy child despite everything I experienced. But that wouldn't be the truth. I had a wonderful childhood, and I don't even remember feeling different or odd constantly going to therapy. My mom installed therapy nets in the playroom, and many of these tools just became playtime to both my sister and to me. It was my normal and often fun.

To be honest, this world is hard for me. And while my story has a happy ending, my journey has been difficult. I would desperately like to tell you not to worry and to be inspired, but I can't overstate the daily difficulty. Even as someone who "made it," because you never truly "make it." The challenges of autism never completely go away, no matter how well you cope.

I was fortunate to grow up when I did, not that it was easy but I had opportunities that children who came before me did not. I was not shipped off after my diagnosis; rather I was given the opportunity to enter this world. This was a new way of thinking. Autism was still a taboo word. I grew up learning to hide my autism and to not tell anyone who did not need to know, for fear doors would be shut before I even had the chance to try. I worked very hard to prove the doctors wrong.

Each time I was told I would never accomplish something, I felt a fire burn inside of me. A determination to do what I was told I could not.

It probably goes without saying that this is an exhausting way to live. Constantly proving that you are capable, constantly hiding your true self. This world is not designed to accurately test the true intelligence of an autistic person.

Working twice as hard to get the same results in an arena not designed for your brain. Hoping to succeed anyway.

I took the SAT three times before my math score was high enough to be considered for college, even though I had a stellar academic record. I was denied testing accommodations on a state bar exam, despite countless documentation. I took my driving test multiple times because spatial relations are so unattainable for me. Each of these times I could have given up. I maybe even wanted to. I was tired, and just for once, I wanted to be able to walk through a door as easily as everyone else.

I had to find strength deep within me. I had to dig down and keep going, knowing I am just as worthwhile as everyone else. Each and every day, I must decide to keep trying.

In my adult life it is still daunting to be completely exposed and known as someone who is autistic. Times have changed, and the world is more accepting but hiding parts of you in exchange for opportunity is a daily challenge. Part of me wonders how much the world truly has changed.

Would I still be judged if the first and only thing someone knew about me was my autism – before seeing my ability?

I wish I had the confidence to say *"no, it wouldn't matter."*

I've studied this world's social games for a long time now. I've seen the patterns, and patterns are hard to break. Eventually this way of life becomes automatic.

No matter how many social cues I memorize, how well I mask, or how many people I accurately recognize without being able to see faces due to being face blind, I will never have the ease of daily life that others experience. I will always be drifting in this storming sea. The difference now is that I can hide it. A skill that's resulted in my independence. It has allowed me to walk through many doors, but it also has its dangers. I must remain vigilant.

I leave you with a question to which I still have not found an answer. I do not know if an answer exists. I challenge you to think of your own truth to this question.

Why are these social constructs so important to you?

4

MARY LYNN

Daily living posed problems in the first two years. Mikhaela could not stand the car or the car seat. She would scream in hysterics the entire trip. Gravitational insecurity was not an understood concept at the time. We now know that simply placing something under the feet will prevent dangling and resolve gravitational insecurity. There were a very limited number of foods that she could tolerate. Mikhaela primarily existed on breast milk until the age of seven months. At this point she turned away from the intensity of nursing. She did continue to nurse in the wee hours of the night when exhaustion had set in. Daytime feedings were replaced with soy formula. Although I made attempts to transition her to solid food, texture seemed to be a huge obstacle. As Mikhaela approached her third birthday, her diet consisted of soy formula and little else. The pediatrician was concerned that she continually flirted with the bottom of the growth chart. Brushing teeth was a monumental task. This led to still more trips to various doctors to determine what type of gastrointestinal issues might be present. Once again, testing offered no answers.

Everyone involved was becoming more and more frustrated, which made me more and more determined to help my little one. By the age of three, Mikhaela possessed very little language using only about 12 to15 words, and no sentences nor stringing words together. The decision was made to treat the symptoms. The first order of business was a hearing evaluation and speech therapy.

The hearing evaluation was a disaster. Mikhaela could not stand to have anything placed on her ears, so a technique was tried where sounds were introduced from various directions in the room. If she responded correctly, a toy clown would clap his hands and light up. This onslaught of sensory input caused Mikhaela to scream. What was intended as a reward had turned to sheer torture. The test did reveal, however, that her hearing was normal. Time for speech therapy.

During college, I had worked with deaf children, and I remembered the criticality of language development. I began signing to Mikhaela in effort to reach into this child and provide her a way into the world. I knew she was in there. I labeled everything in the house with its proper name, for example, the label "CHAIR" was attached to all of the chairs and "TABLE" to all tables and so on.

Mikhaela loved the bathtub. She relaxed there, so I used that time to try to teach her new signs.

To my utter disappointment, she responded to none of these techniques. It was at this time that I began to realize that there was some sort of a processing problem. I just didn't have a clue what it could be. Nor did anyone else.

The speech therapist in San Francisco, where we lived at the time, thought there might be an attentional issue because Mikhaela had severe gaze aversion. To be honest I was ready to latch on to anything that might hold the key. My gut told me this was different from ADD. Mikhaela could and often did become fixated on things or activities for long periods of time. Even at this tender age, she lined up toys and had a profound need for things to be in a specific place. She would spend hours repeatedly watching the same videos. Play dates with children her own age were impossible. Either there was no interaction, or she wanted to control all aspects of the game. Sharing was not a concept she could grasp.

There was, however, wonderful one-on-one time with my daughter during this period. She loved the zoo, and we spent many days there walking and wandering. The best part being no rules for social interaction. Mikhaela was free to be herself. She also loved the beach, or I should say she loved the ocean. The water in San Francisco is too cold too swim, so it would not be until years later that I would discover that she could not tolerate the salt water. Of course, the sand was an issue from the start. No sand castles for this little girl. These outings provided relief from the testing and the therapy and allowed Mikhaela and I to begin to develop a bond that would see us both through the trying times that lay ahead. It also provided space for her to be a child in her own unique way.

It was around this time Mikhaela started to exhibit some other odd behaviors. She toe-walked. She spun. She spent hours in her closet playing with her favorite toys called Polly pockets. She rocked. She flapped her hands and tugged at her ears. I remember distinctly our neighbor giving Mikhaela the nickname "Minnie Mouse."

I was thrilled the time Mikhaela looked up at me and recited the entire "Snow White" video. I mean all of it, including the dwarf dialogue. I thought, "Yes! We finally have language!!" What she had was a phenomenal memory. By four years of age, she had been through speech therapy, occupational therapy, and physical therapy for a variety of problems ranging from coordination issues to muscle weakness. We had moved to North Carolina, and we were still unable to find a pediatrician, expert of any kind, or person on the planet that could do more than just treat the symptoms.

Mikhaela had enough language that I thought it would be a good idea to try preschool. After all, isn't that what four-year olds do? It was a half-day program several days a week. Half day meaning two hours. I always picked up Mikhaela before playground time. She simply wasn't capable of social interaction. Besides, she was exhausted from two hours of masking and trying to hold it together. Never mind the extreme meltdown that occurred daily when I put her in the car to come home. She was in preschool. That was a success in my book.

Then came the big blow. I was called in to see the teacher. I was nervous. My mind raced.

What had happened?

As I sat in a chair designed for five-year olds, my five-foot ten-inch frame ached from the anxiety. I suddenly felt small. The middle-aged teacher looked over the top of red-framed glasses and said,

"I have some concerns about your daughter."

Who didn't?

The rest of the conversation is a blur. There was something about being outside the parameters of typically developing children her age, inability to use scissors, or understand colors, and poor social skills. I agreed to have her tested once again. This meeting paled in comparison to the phone call I would receive the following year from the same school asking me to pick up Mikhaela because she was licking the walls. What difference did that make? After all, she wasn't licking the other children, was she?

5

MIKHAELA

So many times I wished I had the words to tell my mom what was wrong when I melted down. Why do I injure myself? What is causing me to be so inconsolable? The truth is, I never knew. I did not realize that the sensory overload was not the same for everyone else, so I did not have the words or awareness to describe what was happening at that young age. I would often bang my legs against tables until I bruised or bang my head in a desperate attempt to rid myself of the sensory onslaught and regain focus and control. Perhaps if I pinched myself hard enough, the swirling colors and lights would fade away.

Without a way to regulate what I was experiencing, I felt helpless. I melted down. The more I tried to suppress the sensory input during the day, the worse my meltdowns became once I was in a safe space. The social nuances and sensory overload were attacking me from all directions.

I can always feel the meltdown coming. I fist

my hands as a release of this tension but it is usually not enough. I become more and more agitated until eventually my anxiety feeds itself and there is no turning back. Once I am melting down it is difficult to regain control. Because I am not doing it for attention, rather it's my response to painful or offending sensory around me. I did not yet have the tools to manage and calm myself. Even the slightest touch felt painful enough to send me over the edge. My meltdowns occurred the most after school after a day of masking.

To some extent, everyone masks. We all wear different masks for different social situations no matter who we are. For example, the person we present to the world at work is different than who we are in our intimate relationships at home. This is simply a social structure and how people are able to become a part of a larger group.

The difference for me was, I did not inherently know these cues. I could not read other people's masks, and I most certainly did not know how I fit into various social situations.

I was constantly bombarded with sensory overload. By the time I actually had the energy to start noticing people, social groups had already been formed. Everyone else was naturally mirroring. I was documenting, learning, memorizing, and then mirroring. I was taking an extra step than everyone else.

That extra step was suppression.

Imagine a world where you have a radio on high volume with no control or way to turn it down. It is constantly blaring in your ears. Now imagine that you must go to school, work, and go out with friends with this blaring radio playing in your head. No one else can hear it or see it. All they can see is you and any socially unacceptable behavior you do caused by the loud radio in order to deal with it, or in some cases things you miss because the radio drowns out so much around you. And because no one else can hear it, you must suppress your anxiety until you are in a safe place to deal with your emotions from the overload.

For a time, I could do this quite well. I could even achieve a sense of normalcy. I would get out of my head by mirroring the actions of other people, almost forgetting about the radio. But eventually, that radio would get on my last nerve. Eventually, I couldn't take it anymore.

As an autistic child, I had no desire to be a part of a social group or to even have friends. This was true even when I was around other autistic people in social skills groups. I am the perfect example of parallel play. Not caring to associate with anyone no matter who they were, happy in my own world. I could not read the social cues of any person, even those like me. These words will sound sad to some, but I want to assure you I didn't mind not having friends. I am content in my own methodical universe.

I understood the trade-off of having friends. The price for admission was to forever be interpreting a foreign language that would never come naturally to me, no matter how hard I tried. I would be mentally exhausted from both dealing with sensory overload and attempting to interact with other people. I was already expending 100% of my energy on finding ways to be happy and to cope with my "head radio." Now I would have to put in another 100% to socialize and interpret. That's a lot of energy for something I wasn't at all sure I wanted.

Because no type of nonverbal social language is natural to me, I do not have my own. My natural social language is none. That is why I am often unable to use the correct tone or give off a non-verbal signal I did not intend. While I can't interpret it, I still emit body language that you surmise using your own language - leading me to unintentionally convey something nonverbally. In my mind, the signal does not exist.

Something inside drove me to want to learn your language, to understand what I was missing. Maybe I would burn out, but I am human, so I want to be a part of this world.

I started mirroring social interactions and masking my overload. A secret struggle that eventually no one could see. With most of human language being nonverbal, you can imagine just how much information I memorized. Truthfully, I am amazed and thankful that I was blessed with a stellar memory.

However, something strange happened to me the more I masked. Throughout my childhood I was often unhappy because I could not control any sensory input. I melted down regularly as a result. As I mirrored, the benefit was, I was not as focused on the sensory overload. It pulled me out of my overwhelming world, and for just a moment, there were times where masking was so second nature. And in that moment I didn't experience the harder parts of autism.

However, as an adult, I find that when I am stressed or overly tired, I can barely contain my overpowering feelings. Oftentimes I have trouble identifying my own needs. I'm left to wonder when my masking container will finally burst. Natural outlets and safe spaces to just be myself are essential.

There have been times when I am unsure of my true personality because I have been mirroring for so long.

What about me is the real me?

Neurotypical children also mirror and copy their friends' interests in development. But here's the key difference: not only was I mirroring, I was not noticing the social cues and was constantly suppressing the overload I felt. That's an exhausting task. And an extra step more than the "normal" social masks typical people may wear everyday. Autistic masking is the masking of our daily overload. Without a safe outlet, this can become dangerous.

I also started to wonder if I was even still autistic because I mask so well. I have masked to the point where I don't even know my own needs sometimes. It's not that I don't struggle enormously with my sensory processing and social communication everyday. It's that I am so good at masking, I have wondered if I even have the same needs for myself as I once did.

Do I deserve support?

Recently, I took another formal test for testing accommodations. Even the person administering it was doubtful, thinking that I was exaggerating. What happened astonished me.

My results were exactly the same as they were when I was 5 years old.

It meant that no matter how well I mask, autism does not disappear. I may trick society into not seeing it, learn every social cue, and even fool myself.

But deep down it's all still there.

All the struggles.

And so thoroughly suppressed that when they burst, it leads to complete burnout.

I do believe it is okay for humanity to mirror each other, behaving in certain ways in specific situations – to an extent. This is how society functions and what makes us civilized. What is difficult is that autistic people do more than that, and not all of us have a safe outlet to be ourselves. That means for some, masking is constant. Additionally, for me, masking is yet another learned skill. This task takes an exorbitant amount of energy. I am not just conforming my behavior to the proper social situation; I am interpreting what behavior to use and simultaneously suppressing my meltdowns.

I do feel I have a real personality even though I learned through mirroring. The things that interested me, I truly like. I picked aspects of people I connected with best to form who I am. In the way many of us do.

I used the mirroring and masking to protect myself from sensory onslaught. Yes, it expends a lot of energy, but everything I do to cope in life requires tremendous amounts of energy. At this point, I don't consider my masks separate from me, just as I don't consider the blaring radio, I can never turn down separate from me. It's all part of who I am. I don't feel fabricated. But I do feel exhausted. And therein lies the concern.

It's what I paid to enter this social world. It would have cost me anywhere in any culture. I could have stayed on the edge of the playground my whole life never noticing another person. I would have been perfectly content, but I took the jump, with both feet, into this world to see what friendships had to offer.

I actually enjoy socializing now, something I never imagined would be possible. I have experienced so much joy I would have missed. I would not trade this for anything.

But it has come at a cost.

I navigate my adult life with care. Ensuring that I do not lose myself within.

I went to an event recently where people knew I was autistic before really knowing me. I had several people remind me who they were because they knew I couldn't recognize faces.

You may not remember me...I know you said it's hard to recognize faces, but I was in your class.

These words meant so much to me. This incredibly simple act made my entire night so much easier and less stressful. Because now I wasn't playing a guessing game, rather people were supporting me. A burden was lifted.

And now I can't help but think, what if that is what it was like for me everywhere? What if instead of me masking all the time, people were able to know to say these simple words to help me navigate social situations? Without judgment, interpreting the language for me. That would be truly freeing.

Perhaps the cost of masking would not be as great if the world were more educated about how best to support autistic people, how to invite us into your world, and how to be a part of ours as well.

Perhaps true acceptance means people accommodating our autistic language.

6

Mary Lynn

By this time, we were burning through pediatricians. This was a frustrating situation for doctors who were overwhelmed by a heavy workload in the world of HMOs. Doctors who truly wanted to help found there were few answers and fewer resources. We made the one and a half-hour journey from Winston-Salem to Durham two to three times a week for therapy. Therapy at the local hospital occurred on the other days as well as at home. A therapy net was installed. Mats went down on the floor.

I tried to make everything fun. This was, after all, still childhood. As it turns out, most children love to swing in a therapy net! This includes siblings and friends.

Although it seemed as though life was revolving around testing and therapy, it was actually marching forward as it does for everyone. My father, the grandfather who first noticed the far away eyes of a new baby girl, was diagnosed with pancreatic cancer and passed away within eight months. He had unknowingly placed his strength, drive, and fire in Mikhaela and that would, in years to come, be the thing that kept all of us going.

His passing on December 20, 1994 yielded to a more joyous occasion. In the middle of grief and chaos, I was blessed with another baby girl. On March 23, Meleana shifted the focus to hope and excitement for the future. The quiet, relentless strength of my mother transformed all the energy and anxiety of the family into forward motion. She became my best friend, and her steady support allowed me to become Mikhaela's best advocate, embodying grace under pressure. She provided the sounding board I needed as well as the financial backing for testing and therapy. By this time, insurance companies were no longer covering any of the expenses. Most still don't.

* * *

It was in Durham that I first heard of a concept called sensory integration. The test used was called SIPT and was given in Durham, then evaluated at UCLA. Again, the meeting to discuss the results became a blur after the first five or ten minutes.

By this time, I had learned to bring my mother to these meetings to serve as a second set of ears. I highly recommend this strategy. Bringing a friend or family member in addition to the parent provides objective feedback and clarification later. Also, have them take notes in the margin of the report. As the parent, you are dealing with so many emotions around your child it is sometimes difficult to comprehend everything when it's happening. These are the times when you are letting go of the hopes and dreams you may have had for your baby and transforming them into realistic goals and expectations. The lesson here is to remember that *all* children with intervention move along the spectrum. Since there is no way to predict how far any child will progress, it is imperative that every child be given the chance to try and possibly succeed through therapy.

Never say never.

The SIPT test revealed that Mikhaela had severe impairment in 15 of the 17 areas of sensory processing. Who knew there were 17 areas of sensory processing? I was taught there were five senses! As usual, I found myself on a learning curve. At least now we had an explanation for some of the behaviors. One of the areas of concern was gravitational insecurity. This refers to an abnormal fear of ordinary movement, having ones feet off the ground, or not being in an upright position. It is what caused her to meltdown in the car seat. She could not stand to have her feet off the ground. It is also what caused her to wake often in the night and why, as a baby, she could only sleep in the snuggly. Today, children use weighted vests, blankets, and even ball caps to combat this problem. Of course, the SIPT also confirmed things I already knew.

Mikhaela could not stand noise, light, or certain textures against her skin. And although she would give a hug, touching was out as a general rule. These deficits in sensory integration caused compensating behaviors such as spinning and toe-walking.

It was about this time when the word "autism" first entered our vocabulary. In the middle 1990's, this was a very scary word indeed. To all who heard it, autism equaled "Rain Man."

In an odd way, I felt relief. At least I knew what we were up against, or so I thought. As it turned out, the diagnosis did not bring strategies to fix it. Mikhaela continued to move into uncharted waters. The DSM changed the diagnostic code in 1990, and Mikhaela was in the first wave of treating these children in a new way. When she was diagnosed, Yale informed me that autism was identified in about 1 out of every 2,000 children in the US. Today that number is 1 out of 59 and boys are four times more likely to be diagnosed.

Against the advice of all who worked with Mikhaela, I enrolled her in first grade in a typically-developing classroom. I was warned that I was setting her up for failure, and that I was a terrible mother for placing her in an environment where she could not possibly succeed. Warnings I had heard before.

A prominent neurologist had tested her and informed me that she would never tie her shoes, ride a bike, or go to school. He said that I just needed to accept this and look for a group home where she would eventually live.

Professionals working with Mikhaela only saw her for short periods of time. I was with her all day. I knew she was there, and I knew she was capable. I knew the determination that was within.

7

MIKHAELA

All I can focus on is the itching and sensory overload of individual electrode monitors as the doctors place them on my scalp. They are gooey and sticky. My head is wrapped to keep them in place. I feel like I have a helmet on my head with all of this around my scalp.

My room is just like any other hospital room. Sterile, white, and the usual hospital smell. I hear the hum of the florescent lights and the whirring of machinery. My mother never leaves my side. She never does. Every so often, someone comes in to check on me. They are reading my brainwaves. I think I hear something about monitoring for potential seizures. I do not really understand what that is, but it sounds serious.

There is also a camera. During a check in, my nurse and I are sitting behind the couch on the floor. The camera begins to move. She waves at it. "They can't see us, it's trying to find where we are," she says. The camera finally sees her waving and stops. Now I have a fun game. I try to hide from the camera to make it move.

A boy is staying in the room across from me. He has the same helmet head look and is about my age. We are both so young but I've only seen children in this area. Every day I go to my doorframe and he goes to his. We play catch. I'm not one for socializing, but he seems nice and he distracts me from the sensory nightmare on my head. We cannot move too far outside our doors because we are attached to monitoring devices.

I try to scratch my head, hoping to take off this helmet. I hope they find what they are looking for. Days pass. Throwing the ball with the boy across the hallway becomes my new preferred routine. It gives me structure and play in this strange place.

I do not sleep well. But who does in hospitals? I wonder if the boy and others are here for the same tests.

I wake up one day to hear the doctors talking to my mom. The next thing I know, they tell me I am being released and the helmet is coming off. I am ecstatic. Not caring to know the results, my world only consists of getting off this helmet of sensory bombardment.

As it is removed, I feel relief. My hair is messy and sticky. I am excited to wash it. We are given the good news that I do not have seizures. When we leave the hospital, I briefly wonder what became of the little boy. We were not able to play the last day. I believe he left before I did. Or maybe he was still there but couldn't come play that day. Is he sicker than I am? I wonder if he is okay, if he has been released like me. I never find out the answer.

I leave not knowing what's ahead of me, leaving my game of catch behind. Wishing that I could have had another social interaction. Feeling for the first time, connected to someone I didn't really know at all.

"How can this be?"

8

Mary Lynn

First grade began. We still commuted on Fridays to Durham for therapy. Mikhaela's eating issues were improving, if only slightly. She ate cheese and mustard sandwiches exclusively for the entire school year.

I hire tutors. I tried to facilitate her social development by showing up at recess with bubbles and chalk for the children. I volunteered for field trips or events that might cause stress for Mikhaela.

A school tradition, where Mikhaela was enrolled, dictated that first graders visit the circus when it came to town. Of course, I helped to chaperone. It was one of the worst outings to date. The flashing lights, loud noises, and large crowd all came together to cause a meltdown of major proportion. Luckily, I had driven my own car and we were able to leave quickly. To this day, Mikhaela despises clowns (as do millions of others).

At Christmas time, Mikhaela became very ill. It started as what we assumed was a simple stomach virus. Eventually she was vomiting every 15 minutes. She became dehydrated and was hospitalized. Again, extensive testing revealed nothing. She slowly regained her health and was released after five days. It was a scary time and a reminder that her health was always in a precarious state.

When summer arrived and first grade was over, it was a tremendous relief. The girls and I spent summer vacations on Lake Norman. The pace was definitely unhurried and allowed everyone to re-charge. Mikhaela had attended first grade in a neighboring city, and we were now looking forward to her beginning second grade in Winston-Salem. The school chosen was one my brother had attended and had a stellar reputation for meeting every child wherever they may be, where everybody can be a somebody.

Once again, the cost was almost prohibitive, but I knew Mikhaela needed an environment where she could lead with her strengths. The school had a waiting list and it was her sister, Meleana, entering kindergarten that paved the way. When Meleana was accepted, her sibling Mikhaela was accepted also!

Through the excitement, I worried. As is my style, I decided to take action. I met with the second-grade teacher at the end of the summer and tried to describe Mikhaela.

I began with the strengths.

Incredibly strong vocabulary and verbal skills had emerged along with fierce determination. Her verbal IQ had tested in the superior range. She was eager to apply any strategies given to her.

I then addressed the deficits.

Her math ability was incredibly weak. In fact, the IQ test indicated a 70-plus point gap. She still struggled with motor coordination, including handwriting. I gently educated the teacher about sensory integration. I informed her about strategies Mikhaela could use if she became overwhelmed, such as pushing against a wall.

The second-grade teacher was enthusiastic about working with Mikhaela, and she was a math expert to boot! I felt we were truly blessed.

As it turned out, Mikhaela refused to use any coping strategies and did not want anyone to even know about her issues. She was determined to handle school just like any other kid.

Second grade offered some unique opportunities. Social interaction remained difficult for Mikhaela, and it was now compounded by the fact that she became aware that she could not make friends. Her teacher continued to be supportive both academically and socially. She would become Mikhaela's first academic champion. Reading started to really take off and was encouraged. This was the first sign that reading was to become a huge part of life. It became ever more apparent that math skills were in the bucket. Due to this teacher's style, frustration rarely set in.

In the spring, the children participated in Native American Day. This event, and all that led up to it in the curriculum, played to Mikhaela's strengths. The only problems were the hand-eye coordination needed for basket weaving and, of course, the itchy costume. I remedied this by placing a soft cotton shirt underneath.

Second grade ended successfully. She made her first holy communion at our church. We entered a period of relative calm. And it was time to return to the lake.

Tutoring and therapy continued through the summer. I also incorporated therapy at the lake. Mikhaela loved body crashing which is the act of seeking out activities that give the body a deep pressure sensation. During the winter months, she had stayed outside sledding in the snow long after the other children had gone inside to warm up. I purchased a towable tube and pulled Mikhaela and Meleana around the lake all summer. We loved swimming. Mikhaela would spend hours lining up toys. It was at this time I began to notice that Mikhaela could tolerate cold much better than heat. She still has difficulty with body temperature regulation. This was yet another unexpected "side effect" of autism.

Meltdowns were also still an issue when overwhelmed. It was like a freight train. I could see it coming, but I couldn't stop it.

We utilized all the strategies learned in therapy. Chewing something hard, chewing something sour, taking a bath, rolling a therapy ball up and down the body to provide pressure. All of these techniques were employed. Sometimes it worked, but oftentimes it didn't.

Mikhaela was also becoming frustrated. She began to ask questions about why she was different from other children. She wanted to know if she could go to live in Heaven with her grandfather where these problems would not exist. She wanted to know why it was night, day, night, day. Why couldn't it just be one thing?

And the hardest question was, "why couldn't I fix it?"

I explained to Mikhaela that this was like a puzzle. We would have to collect strategy pieces and try to fit them together. The hard part would be that not all the pieces would fit in her puzzle because everyone is different. We would have to see what fit and use it, and throw the others away. Of course, just like a puzzle, you don't know if the piece fits until you try it because no one has the same puzzle. That does not mean you are broken, it just means you need a different piece. This was, and still is, a painstaking process. Being results oriented, there were profound lessons in patience and process for me. I strongly believe we are given the children from whom we can best learn.

9

MIKHAELA

Sometimes, there are occurrences that remind me that I am not like everyone else. Even when you accommodate yourself so well that you often forget you have any challenges at all. But they are still there.

A lot of times I laugh at such moments. Like when I hear a word completely different from what someone has said. Or when my literal mind misinterprets or cannot understand a joke. Other times, I feel small and defeated. Fully realizing that in some ways I am disabled and not like everyone else. I'm the person who will wander in circles for hours trying to find a location even if I am less than a mile away, my brain unable to understand how to find a new way there if my route had to change. Or looking at numbers on a board being so close to understanding the math concept, and even seeing how it would make sense to other people, but never being able to fully make the connection.

However, I have many favorite parts about

autism. One of my favorite things about being autistic is how literal I am. I believe I pick up on more information because I am not distracted by social cues. Because I cannot sense "vibes" in a room or read facial expressions, I am rarely fazed during a presentation. Routine makes me more productive as well.

I also always wanted to be the best both in academics and in my therapy. I felt that since I am so uncomfortable and unsure socially, I want to be the best at everything else. To feel worthy, I realize now I often don't give myself enough credit. But it's hard to break the cycle of comparing yourself to other people when you have taught yourself to mirror others your whole life. I put my full effort into therapy. I wanted to prove everyone wrong. I wanted to succeed. I still want to succeed.

Life was not always easy. Dry brushing is a sensory integration therapy. It felt very painful at the time even though it was only a light touch for a few minutes every two hours. However, I am glad I did it because I can now be touched without feeling pain. It is interesting to me how I can feel no pain when I am injured, yet the slightest touch has the ability to send sharp sensations throughout my body.

I learned how to make sensory input more accessible for me. I wear clothes that cling to my whole body, avoiding anything that is clingy in one part but not another. I like to feel the same consistency throughout, as if it is a second skin. It needs to be the same amount of pressure in all places. Tights are a nightmare because they are tighter on my legs than the rest of my clothes. I can tell if I will be able to tolerate something just by touching the fabric.

And, of course, no tags!

I keep lights dim in my room and avoid fluorescents in my own space. I use noise-cancelling headphones, and don't accept invitation to places I know will end in sensory overload (like loud concerts and bars). Many times, I am the one that initiates a social invitation. This gives me complete control because I'm able to pick the social activity and how many people to invite. I often pick activities I already enjoy with one or two people. This allows me to be calmer, because it is something I am already fond of doing, and I feel more natural. Eventually, I begin to associate the friend I invite with the calming activity. The socialization then becomes less of a burden and something to which I actually look forward.

I don't make eye contact for long periods of time and instead look at the forehead or someone's mouth.

Most importantly, I have learned to self-advocate. I have realized that just because everyone else's way doesn't always work for me, I'm not any less intelligent or have any less potential. Just as no autistic person is the same, no neurotypical person is the same. We all have unique strengths and weaknesses. It is how we utilize our strengths that determines our success. And each person's success will look different because we all have unique gifts to share with this world. No person will ever have the same story or same ending, but we can still be equally happy. That is true grace.

10

MARY LYNN

The therapist in Durham had been using a technique called cranial sacral therapy. When I first saw it, it looked to be very suspect. Basically, it utilizes pressure applied by the hands about the gram weight of a nickel. The premise is to relieve pressure that may be present in the fascia of the skull and sacral regions. Since I had adopted a philosophy that if it can't hurt, and it might help, let's try it. We did. Mikhaela responded beautifully, almost miraculously. We attended an intensive clinic in Florida that yielded incredible results. For the first time, Mikhaela had a voracious appetite. She was trying all kinds of food.

There was another benefit.

Mikhaela had never had good pain reception. She had once slammed her thumb in the car door and didn't even shed a tear. We went on to dinner and as I watched the swelling mount, we were off to the emergency room. She had indeed shattered the bones in her thumb. After this cranial sacral clinic, the pain receptors were working. This proved to be the most helpful therapy with all regulatory issues. Although this is one of those things about which many are skeptical, I can tell you that it worked for Mikhaela. I must point out, however, that I also took Meleana for cranial sacral work for issues that were arising in her, and it yielded no results. Like many things in life, what works for one person may not work for another.

Meleana had developed an incredible wit and this proved to be an invaluable asset to Mikhaela as well as the whole family. We spent the summer reading *Amelia Bedelia* and working on idioms, inference, and innuendo. These are concepts that remain difficult even now. Meleana also began to cue Mikhaela naturally. A better sister could not have been designed. Meleana was extraordinarily patient and used humor to take the stress out of intense situations.

It was time for third grade. During this school year, Mikhaela's insatiable appetite for reading developed. Math was still an extraordinary struggle, but reading was taking off. It was difficult to keep up with her. I found it amazing then, as I do now, that a brain can be positively brilliant in one area and so utterly incapable in another. Multiplication tables reared their ugly head for the first time, and it became more apparent that any linear thinking was out of the question. Telling time and counting money still continue to present a challenge in Mikhaela's daily living skills. Reading provided the escape that kept Mikhaela sane. She was also developing a love of writing.

Once again, a teacher, actually two, stopped me in the school hallways. When asked if I was Mikhaela's mother, I panicked slightly.

What now?

My mind was immediately sent careening back to every evaluation or meeting to discuss my daughter's issues. I braced, ready to quickly find the answer to whatever was the current concern. I noticed my mouth was dry and the pace of my heart quickened.

To my utter surprise, these teachers wanted to convey how WELL Mikhaela was doing in writing! That was it! I couldn't believe it.

I cried all the way home in the car.

As luck would have it, one of these teachers would continue to work with and follow Mikhaela throughout her elementary and junior high career. She found Mikhaela fascinating. She relished in her strengths and continued to teach her to lead with them. This is a great strategy for all students. Become competent in your weak areas and lead with your strengths.

Social skills were still presenting problems. The playground was difficult, and she still did not have any real friends. Social skills groups and comic strip stories were invaluable. Comic strip conversations give a visual representation to help clarify social understanding. We continued to work on literal thinking and idioms. She is the only child I know who looked up when told, *"when pigs fly."* Even now this type of language is very difficult, if not impossible. A common refrain is "say what you mean and mean what you say!"

Other milestones were reached at the end of third grade. After intensive therapy, Mikhaela acquired better motor skills and learned to ride a bike. Meltdowns continued at home, but she was able to keep it together in school and in public for the most part. She had successfully participated in Pioneer Day at school. Her love of rules made her an easy student to handle. Routine became her savior. As long as life was predictable, she did well. The moment things were out of order, chaos reigned. Thankfully, it was time to return to the lake.

11

MIKHAELA

Rigid behavior is not something I enjoy, but is a way for me to feel I can survive in a world where I am constantly out of control. I do not have command over my emotions, sensory regulation, or knowledge of social cues. Predictability enables me to know what to expect in different scenarios and prepare myself for the experience. Because of this need for predictability I often felt held back both in what activities I could participate and in my human relationships. It was difficult for me to connect to other people. Because people after all, are the definition of unpredictable, especially when you don't know how to interpret their behaviors. It should not come as a surprise then, that what helped me step outside myself and become calmer in the face of unpredictability was a steady energy. Animals.

When I was in early elementary school my family decided to get a therapy dog for me. The dog would help me with emotional attachment, calming, and stability. To say the least, I wasn't thrilled by the idea. At this point I didn't attach well emotionally to either people or pets. I liked animals, but not near me. I did not want them touching me or coming too close. I truly preferred my own isolated world, devoid of people or animals.

My mom made a big deal about the dog to get me excited. I did not even want to go and pick him out. Instead, I opted to help pick out the crate, dog toys, dog bed, and other things he would need. I have always preferred objects and find solace in creating my own world with objects. My sister went with my mom to pick the dog. We got a black lab mix because labs are supposed to be a great breed for training to be a therapy dog. However, the dog my family picked was very high energy. He ended up failing out of dog therapy school. He simply wasn't the correct temperament. I was initially not thrilled by my new high-energy addition. Little did I know how much he would change my life, even though he was not an official therapy dog.

I named the dog Milo because I had just read *The Phantom Tollbooth* in which the main character goes by the same name. Milo was slobbery, high energy, always in my space, all the things that I didn't like. But all the things I needed. A calmer dog would have been good for me. However, I think I was meant to have Milo. He pushed me outside my comfort zone. And showed me how to enter a different world I'm not usually willing to try. Eventually, he showed me how to attach emotionally.

Milo, although hyper, provided the calm energy I needed to reset. For me, all people give off energy. This energy drains me because I can feel it constantly even if I cannot identify what it is exactly. With Milo, he did not have any of this energy. He was just a clean slate. There were no secret nonverbal languages being spoken, even his eyes were less intense to me because they did not portray the complexity of human eyes. The emotions he had were simply those of joy. He was a positive light and I could feel my own negative emotions calming when I was near him. As if his light was in some way washing out the dark energy building up inside of me, giving me a breath of fresh air. I have always felt this way in nature as well.

Milo always stayed near to me, no matter how much I didn't want him. He especially stayed near to me through all of my childhood illnesses, of which there were many. He was a loyal presence, patiently waiting for me to be ready. Slowly, but surely, I began to bond with Milo. Over time, I became completely attached.

I was so attached that I even began to stim on Milo. Rubbing his ears or rubbing my nose through his fur over and over became my go to stims. And Milo never minded. In fact, he enjoyed it and often approached me to have his ears rubbed. However, looking back there became points where I was too attached. I began to love Milo more than I cared for people.

This was one of my first emotional attachments. Now that I had experienced it, I could transfer to people and human friendships. I took the same lessons I had learned from Milo and the same feelings to use in my friendships. He taught me what emotional attachment feels like and what friendship has to offer.

I will never have another dog like Milo because Milo was no ordinary pet. Though he was never officially my therapy dog by certification that is what he became. He provided a bridge to this world for me. I truly believe animals have the ability to know our souls and give us what we need, even if we do not know what we need ourselves. I would not have the same capability to make friendships as well as I do without him or the awareness of my own emotional self. He brought me out of the cognitive and logical world in which I am most comfortable and into the realm of emotions where I was scared to venture. He guided me, at my own pace, allowing me to see what it had to offer and how to navigate it. While patterns and routines are comfortable, I now know I am fully capable of dealing with matters of the heart, despite how difficult it is for me to identify my own emotions due to the intensity I experience.

Milo showed unconditional love and patience, something we all need and was instrumental for me as an autistic child. Though I received this from my family, I did not always know how to read it. Animals are much easier to read than humans, and they are nothing but genuine. This makes the transition to reading people just a little easier. As I grew to understand this, I relied on Milo less and less and more on my human relationships.

Thank you to Milo for everything you gave me. Even though I didn't want a dog, you became everything I needed. You became my first friend.

12

MARY LYNN

It was during the summer prior to fourth grade that I realized just how difficult life had become for Mikhaela. The meltdowns were still an issue most days. I had fought placing my daughter on medication though it had been suggested since the age of four. I was now painfully watching Mikhaela as she desperately tried to fight off the inevitable meltdowns using the strategies she had been taught in therapy.

In conjunction with her pediatrician, I began to explore the pharmaceutical options. Many medications were suggested ranging from anti-seizure meds to psychotropics. I knew she did not have seizures because of our time in a seizure unit at the request of the neurologist during the days of grabbing at straws.

And, of course, she was not psychotic.

I decided to treat the most offending symptoms. These were the things that interfered most with daily life. As I considered this approach, I realized that the need for sameness and getting stuck repeating the same thing over and over was similar in nature to Obsessive Compulsive Disorder. The need to repeat (called echolalia) is still present in Mikhaela today, though to a much lesser extent.

I decided to try an SSRI called Luvox that had been developed specifically to treat OCD. After all, I did not want to change who she was, I just wanted to make her life easier. After several weeks of trying to find the correct dose, Mikhaela became a much happier child. Luvox, and later Lexapro, offered relief from the anxiety and the intense need for ritual. As all medications do, it also came with a price. Nightmares were a nasty side effect for the duration. We were eventually able to discontinue medication in high school.

The other piece of the puzzle that came along that year was a trip to the Yale Child Study Center arranged by the pediatrician. It consisted of testing over a three-day period by a team of specialists. These doctors were the pioneers, and are now leaders, in the field of autism. Again, the cost was brutal. In addition to the cost of testing, there were the expenses of transportation and lodging. Later visits to the center would thankfully include lodging at the Ronald McDonald House. I cannot adequately express my gratitude to the Ronald McDonald House. It is difficult enough to have a child who is experiencing medical problems without having to worry about a place to stay. The staff is supportive beyond belief.

Mikhaela went with the team for the various testing. I was questioned extensively about the pregnancy, labor and delivery, and every moment of her childhood that I could remember. When it was all said and done, we went home and waited for the report to arrive. Six weeks later, we received a roadmap that was twenty pages long. It included learning strategies that I couldn't wait to try. I immediately made an appointment with the teacher. It was midyear of Mikhaela's fourth grade schoolyear.

Once again, Mikhaela had been blessed with an incredible teacher. He was young and energetic and willing to try new ideas. We met and discussed the report as it applied to education. A valuable lesson learned is to not overwhelm teachers with lengthy medical reports. Try to sift through and find the most import and pressing needs of the moment. Then advocate for those strategies. In this case, we decided to focus on Mikhaela's inability to transfer knowledge from one setting to another and to find the most salient point.

This teacher made it his job to teach these skills in the classroom as well as other settings at school as they presented themselves. One day, the teacher decided to change the seating arrangement in his classroom. He took great care not to move Mikhaela's desk, but he did move all the other desks. This undid his young autistic student. When Mikhaela came home terribly upset about the matter, I decided she was old enough to begin advocating for herself. She was extremely nervous, so I agreed to go with her, but she would have to do the talking.

Of course, we were all on the learning curve, but it was a momentous occasion. Mikhaela actually stated the problem, expressed her anxiety, and waited for a response. The teacher understood her concern, and a decision was made to leave things as they were and to help Mikhaela with the new configuration. What a great life lesson. Although the teacher was sensitive to her needs, sometimes she needed to adapt to the surroundings.

Mr. Mac became a favorite teacher and developed a friendship/mentor relationship that continued into adulthood. It is important for autistic kids, and all kids for that matter, to develop relationships with people outside the family upon whom they can rely for direction and feedback.

The other saving grace to develop during fourth grade was Mikhaela's continuing love of reading. Mr. Mac noticed that she was rarely without a book. Although reading probably provided an escape from the demands of social situations, I soon made the connection that this was another intense interest. It had taken the place of stimming during the school day.

Physical directions have always been a challenge. One day Mr. Mac called me at home. No worries needed, Mikhaela was okay. My mind began to race. To encourage her independence, he had allowed her to go to the library alone. Of course, she lost her way. She spent an hour wandering around until another school employee noticed and helped her back to her classroom. Crisis averted. Thank goodness for GPS so she can navigate as an adult.

13

Mikhaela

I am in a new place. It's cold and grey in this state. I like it.

We are in a house with other people. They call it the Ronald McDonald House. I am here for more testing. We share it with other families who also need a place to stay. I very much enjoy this house. It has rules, structure, routine, and everyone had an assigned job. We even have designated times of the day to perform these jobs and charts. Heaven!

Doctors show me different pictures of faces while I am in a giant loud machine. They want me to tell them differences in the faces.

How silly, can't they see that all of these faces are the same? Eyes, nose, mouth, what more could you need?

They want to know facial expressions. I have questions.

Why would a smile mean anything different than happy? Why would a person be sad if there are no tears? Why would they not just tell you they are sad?

I am asked to do puzzles to measure something else. I really dislike puzzles. I cannot visualize how different shapes will fit together or look in a space.

We travel home.

At home I participate in social groups and other therapy. My favorite is the therapy nets, jumping on trampolines and mats, and other activities like horse back riding. I connect with the animals; they are easier to read than people. They don't give off the same energy as a person, just a calming blank slate that I can reset when I'm around them.

My least favorite therapies are motor skills like learning to tie shoes. I have Velcro shoe straps. Why do I need this skill? Holding pencils also seems to be a frustrating task. I don't enjoy learning the social sillies, the nickname therapists give to neurotypical social cues and nonverbal social rules. We call them social sillies because they really are quite silly and arbitrary. There is no particular reason behind the rules, which makes them difficult to learn. Other people sure live their lives in odd ways. Why beat around the bush in social situations so much? Why is sarcasm funny? Saying something that isn't true that the other person somehow also knows isn't true is apparently a joke. But it is different from a lie. Neurotypicals seem to find the most convoluted ways to relate to each other sometimes. I'll play along.

Turns out you can't copy or mimic a joke. Or sarcasm. Something about tone and delivery, reading the audience. I quickly give up on this. I don't need to be a comedian anyway. I laugh at school when I think someone is telling a joke, hoping I'm correct. I have several teachers who use sarcasm. It's unsettling.

I decide to stick with knock-knock jokes. Those seem logical and orderly.

I walk into school one day to hear the teacher announce that we are moving desks. This is not orderly. I feel panic and terror. I cannot learn if I don't remain in the same seat. I also like the front of the room so as to not be distracted by other students in front of me. I can pretend it is just the teacher and me.

I want my mom to fix this. I tell her the problem. She responds, *"I will help you, but you need to tell him yourself and learn to express the problem."*

This is not the answer I was hoping for. My heart sinks. My mom is the social genius, why can she not just do it for me? There is no way I can do this.

I walk in to the meeting with my strategy. I am extremely nervous, thinking about my tone and my words. I start explaining. To my surprise, the teacher understands and allows me to stay in my seat. The other students will be moved, but I can deal with that. It doesn't matter who sits beside me, I don't recognize their faces anyway.

14

MARY LYNN

By sixth grade we were in a predictable and comfortable school routine, or so I thought. The year started well. Yet again, Mikhaela was fortunate to have not one but two fabulous math teachers, the everyday teacher and one who taught a math lab twice a week. Manipulatives such as clay, blocks, and other hands on tools were used with all of the students. There continued to be a struggle in math and linear thinking but Mikhaela always gave her best effort. One of her teachers had a very dry sense of humor and that really helped her practice non-literal speech and nonverbal cues. Just as we were sailing through sixth grade, another medical crisis occurred. It started as a cold and quickly developed into pneumonia. Mikhaela was at home for a month. I had returned to work part time and it was my mother who stepped in. We worked together to keep her academics on track, and under the grandmother's guidance, Mikhaela produced a fabulous project on the coral reef!

It was during this year that Mikhaela was asked to participate in a face study being conducted by Yale University. We traveled to Connecticut. She was placed in an MRI machine and shown different facial expressions and asked to describe them. Although we were not given her specific results, it is apparent that face blindness was (and still is) a significant obstacle.

15

MIKHAELA

Imagine a world where you cannot recognize the faces of anyone, not even your loved ones. No matter how intently you study the face and try to understand the features, it will not compute into your memory. The face is made up of strange shapes, intense eyes, and variations that are so slight everyone may as well look the same. Going out for any reason is accompanied by the anxiety you may not recognize someone. You are not a shy person by nature, yet you turn into one because you cannot locate who you are looking for when you enter a room. You arrive first so that people will hopefully recognize you instead.

Every social engagement ends in exhaustion. You refrain from using the restroom at a crowded restaurant because you know you will never find your way back to your table or be able to recognize the people at your table.

Always secretly hoping no one leaves, telling you they'll meet you outside, because you know once separated, you won't recognize them easily. Not knowing if someone is related to another because you don't see the intricacies of the facial features that make people look like alike.

I wish I had this capability so that when I have a child, I'll be able to experience the joy of seeing someone who looks like me.

This is my reality.

For me, not being able to recognize faces or facial expressions is one of the hardest parts of autism. It is something I wish I could learn or one day it would just click for me. I see and experience every other sensation, color, and light around me so intensely my mind was never able to absorb the features of a face, making me blind to it. My spatial relations skills test so low that it wouldn't surprise me if that is another reason I am unable to put the shapes of each individual feature together to see a face. No faces. No expressions. Only colors and blurs of people.

When I tell people I cannot recognize them, I am met with odd responses. I will never know how essential and personal it is for their face be recognized. To me, I attach no significance to whether or not I am recognized since I am unable to do this myself. But to others, it's a sense of connection.

Every time I try to recognize a face, or facial expression, it is like trying to read a Chinese character. Maybe if I see Chinese characters often enough

I will learn the language. Or maybe it will always be confusing, and I'll never be able to attach the correct meaning to it.

When I speak with someone, I do see his or her face. I see it like I imagine you would see it. And in the moment, I know who it is. But the minute the person walks away, changes clothes, changes hair color, or sees me in an out of context situation where I am not expecting to meet, it is as if I've never seen this person before.

It is as if my short-term memory is able to see the face but unable to translate the person's face to my long-term memory. Meaning, when I see someone at the grocery store that I normally only see in the office, it is almost certain I will not notice or recognize them because I am not actively looking for them.

To recognize someone, I must be expecting to see them so that I can manually access the other information I have stored in my memory to identify them.

I put a lot of effort into making up for this. Going through life unable to see faces or see emotions and expressions is extremely draining and frustrating. So, I pick up on other things instead. I memorize everything else about a person. The clothes they wear, the way they smell, the hairstyle, voices. And then I fill in the gaps to identify them. I am always doing detective work.

For example, recently I took a standardized licensing exam for my profession. One of my old college mentors was at the exam for her students. There were 600 people walking out of the exam and she was standing at the top of the escalator giving hugs to her students as they exited. I first heard her voice and recognized it. I then looked over. Same height, same color hair and hairstyle, and similar clothes as to what I remembered. I also knew she was now working in this area. But I was not 100% sure. I couldn't recognize the face. If it was the person I thought, then I very much wanted to approach and say hello. Imagine how hard it is looking over at someone and not knowing who they are.

I then have to make a choice: take the gamble, approach, and find a way to play it off if I am wrong, or not approach and risk appearing rude.

In this instance, I really wanted to say hello if it was her. And I had enough to go on that made it a high probability it was the person I thought it was. I decided to say her name.

In this type of situation, the worst-case scenario would be no one responding to the name, and because it was so crowded, I could easily walk away if that happened. I tried it. And as luck would have it, it was her. I got my hello.

What amazed me most after this experience was that so much time had passed, and yet I was still able to use all of the other features I memorized about her to correctly identify who she was even without the face. I truly believe one of the reasons my memory is so excellent is because of things like face-blindness. It has to be good.

Another time my memory made up for my inability to have facial recognition was in college. I was walking to my dorm room and saw a hoop earring on the ground. There was nothing special about it and looked exactly like one any girl could be wearing. I picked up the earring and brought it to the girl I thought it belonged to. I was correct. Out of over 5,000 students I knew which one the earring belonged to because I had memorized every accessory everyone wore in order to recognize them. I knew it was her earring because I had used it to identify her before.

For autistic people like me, changing your style, your hair, or even simple things about your appearance without warning is incredibly difficult. I use all of those things to identify you. It's all I have.

This is not to say don't ever change. While it is important that we adapt, just know this would often be a source of anxiety for me. If someone changes without warning, I lose my ability to recognize that person. For family members or close friends, it is helpful if they warn me before they make a change so that I know what to expect. I can document it into my memory. If meeting somewhere, let me know exactly where you are and pick a place where you are easily visible. Approach me first if I fail to find you.

My coworkers and friends may change appearance often, and there is nothing I can do about that. I have learned effective ways around it. They are effective, but draining. Although most of my masking has become automatic, lack of facial recognition is the one thing I am still very much aware of and struggle with daily. Accessing my other memories of identifiers is not automatic at all but it is taxing. But I have become good at it.

In many cases I prep myself beforehand. I do my research. Do I know what someone is wearing? Do I have a picture I could look at and maybe hope something sticks before they walk in? Do I know where they are sitting or whom they are with?

This world is made up of nonverbal communication as its main language, along with millions of faces. None of which I am able to learn despite my very best efforts.

Know that I do wish I could understand when you are frustrated or sad. I wish I could discern the uniqueness of your face. But in a world where I am overrun by sensory and lack of spatial connection, it leaves me navigating a different path. A path full of swirling colors so bright it hurts, piercing sounds, eyes so intense they bring uneasiness to my soul, and faces so many that I see all yet none.

I am forever navigating without a map. Navigating a faceless world.

16

MARY LYNN

We began Equine Assisted Therapy. The recreational therapist was fabulous, and as it turned out, the horses had a calming effect on Mikhaela. I enrolled both Mikhaela and her sister. They both loved it! Meleana was often included in therapy, hospital and educational settings, as the typically developing child. Consequently, she never saw disability but rather ability.

As a child, her first question was always "do you want to play?" She grew up to be a recreational therapist working in a crisis group home setting for adults with intellectual disabilities and mental illness. Amazing Grace!

As seventh grade approached, so did junior high school. This presented a whole new world of social sillies compounded by the influence of hormones. Simple things like whole rows of lockers were a daunting challenge. Find your locker. Open your locker. Also add to the list changing classrooms for different subjects. This inherently brought a new onslaught of sensory overload, which other students relished.

The chaos of the hallway and lunchroom that is adolescent bliss, was terrifying for Mikhaela. On the other hand, the library was smack dab in the middle of the junior high school building, which provided a much-needed respite for Mikhaela. Junior high also offered the opportunity to participate in plays. It was here where Mikhaela could flourish. It was easy for her to memorize lines, and she could deliver again and again exactly as the director asked.

Unbeknownst to me, this was a result of all of those years of mimicking others' behavior in an attempt to fit in. And because she almost never understood humor, Mikhaela was the perfect straight man for any comedy.

Always play to your strength. And yes, pun intended!

We took seventh and eighth grade day by day. Mikhaela developed a passion for history so I nurtured that with trips to historical houses, landmarks, and museums. Eighth grade brought a major project on the civil war. So off we went to the battlefields of Virginia and Pennsylvania. We tried everyday to stay focused on the positive. If it is difficult to understand and explain the social dynamics of adolescence, it is downright impossible to impart this to a young autistic. Humor was our savior during this time – as it so often can be in many situations.

17

MIKHAELA

Imagine this. You are in a foreign country. You don't know the language let alone the social cues. You are unsure of what responses your nonverbal behaviors will create. The things you thought were friendly, in this culture may be perceived as offensive. Being on the spectrum is like being in a foreign country every hour of every day. One of the reasons I do not get easily frustrated when I travel internationally is because I am always doing detective work, guessing what nonverbal behaviors mean, abroad as well as at home.

Why does it matter if I switch lunch tables in the middle of the school year in middle school? Why would people take offense to me sitting at different tables during the week? Why is anything other than a logical knock-knock joke funny? The world is very confusing to me.

My mind is like a filo-fax of flashcards. For each nonverbal cue, I have a mental flashcard on what it could mean in different scenarios. To me, it means nothing. So, I have memorized what it could mean to other people. A smile means approachability, for example. What does this mean for someone like me? Every single interaction I have during the day I constantly and quickly sift through my mental flashcards, pick the appropriate one based on the situation, and then apply the proper response. The problem comes in when I guess incorrectly.

To me, a smile is a smile. How can I tell the difference between a friendly smile and a flirtatious smile? Well, the eyes. (Want to know a secret? I hate eye contact. Eye contact is too intense for me.)

When I look into someone's eyes I cannot simultaneously process. Everything happening during eye contact is distracting to me and requires too much of my energy. This is especially true with flirtatious eye contact. The more intense the eye contact, the more it makes me feel on edge. It has the ability to send chills down my spine and can make me feel fear. I can't tell you why this is. Maybe for people on the spectrum, that peek into our souls from an outsider's eyes is too much to handle along with the entire external overload. It used to be that even simple eye contact felt this way. It evoked a flight response. Now I can manage everyday eye contact, but I still shrink away from intense eye connection and expressions. Imagine a feeling for you that creates a flight response, whether it be public speaking or going to a medical procedure. That is the level of intensity I feel when met with direct eye contact.

Due to this intensity, I cannot master understanding certain expressions when I see them. I can't study them long enough to make a mental flashcard for every intricacy (which allows me to then accurately place each expression as I see them).

Eyes will always remain mysterious to me. Something that I shy away from. It is not that I do not want to connect with you, but my way with connecting with you is different. I feel closer to people when I'm able to listen without looking at the face or eyes. Just as my empathy is often different than yours, so is my way of expressing human connection.

18

MARY LYNN

In February of eighth grade, Mikhaela had what initially seemed to be some difficulty breathing. The doctor attributed it to asthma and prescribed a treatment of albuterol. Her breathing symptoms calmed. By bedtime, however, she was not feeling well, and her hands were shaking. I wondered if she could be having an adverse reaction to the medication. Nothing could have prepared us for what lay ahead. I awoke to the piercing cries from Mikhaela's room. I dashed to her bedside. She was so frightened she could barely tell me the problem. It turns out with very good cause. What came next took my breath away.

My fourteen-year old daughter could not lift her arms. She could not make a fist. When I attempted to help her out of the bed, it became painfully obvious that she could not bear weight on her legs. We were both terrified.

My mother and I somehow managed to get her into the car, and I sped to the emergency room.

She was seen right away. A barrage of testing ensued, including blood work, a CAT scan, and evaluations from many specialties. Unfortunately, there was not a pediatric neurologist available. We were given the option of being admitted to the hospital or going home and returning for additional testing during the week. I opted to go home. I felt the stress of being in a hospital setting would only serve to make things worse. The bombardment of sensory stimulus is difficult for many patients who don't have autism. For Mikhaela, even the hum of the florescent lights is deafening.

Once home, the reality set in. Mikhaela needed help with everything from bathing to feeding. She was frantic. I remained strong and reassuring in her presence but cried myself to sleep at night. What in the world was happening? Hadn't she been through enough? As always, it was my faith that saw me through and allowed me to stay strong. For that, I will be forever grateful. No matter the challenge, God has us in the palm of His hand.

I phoned a dear friend of mine, who was a doctor (and one of my father's former tennis partners). He had helped through my dad's illness and death and was very willing to help in any way possible in this situation. He spoke to a colleague who was a neurologist for adults but agreed to see Mikhaela as a favor. We arrived at the appointed time hoping this man held the answer. She could now just bear weight on her legs but could hardly walk. She had regained the use of her hands, but they were still weak. Another alarming symptom had emerged. In her field of vision everything below about the level of a light switch appeared in her eyes to be leaning to the left.

The neurologist examined her thoroughly. He reviewed the test results from the hospital. It had been suggested that perhaps this was Guillain Barre Syndrome, a condition that causes paralysis caused by the immune system. He dismissed that and did not hesitate with a diagnosis. It was cerebellar ataxia caused by the Epstein-Barr virus.

What did that mean?

He explained that the virus had settled in the cerebellum, the part of the brain that controls motor function. And while she would not deteriorate any further, he was not at all sure she would improve. The virus explained her severe fatigue, its hallmark calling card. At least that would improve over time. Mikhaela could not attend school. She was exhausted most of the time and that carried on until the end of summer. By the end of March, Mikhaela could go to school for about three hours a day. The school was extremely supportive. Lessons were sent home, and I began homeschooling. Her vision continued to pose a problem. While at school, Mikhaela would often run into walls.

Eventually she just began to walk along the wall feeling her way.

I met with the head of school worried she would not be able to complete eighth grade. In keeping with the spirit of the school's mission, the faculty met her where she was and helped her through. Once again, I felt grateful in a way I could not adequately express. This health challenge left her painfully thin and weak.

In May, Mikhaela made her confirmation in our church reminding us once again that God is good.

We returned for a follow up visit with the neurologist in June, and he told us that whatever deficits Mikhaela currently experienced were not likely to improve. We needed to accept her limitations and put supports in place. I had certainly heard that before in raising this child. As luck would have it, I was attending an autism support group meeting and another parent mentioned a doctor who was using a hyperbaric chamber to treat autistic patients. Maybe this could help heal Mikhaela's brain. This doctor had treated her before for digestive issues and discovered that she was lacking certain enzymes. I felt it was certainly worth a try. We had nothing to lose.

Once again, the treatment was expensive and not covered by insurance. The doctor recommended a series of ten hyperbaric chamber dives lasting 45 minutes, once a week. She also suggested a special diet high in zinc and other nutrients known to help the brain. The whole family embraced the process and the diet. Once more my mother came to the rescue providing the needed funding, and of course, led the cheering section. Sure enough, I thought we were beginning to see small improvement about four weeks into the treatment.

I didn't dare allow myself to get too hopeful, but I remained cautiously optimistic. In August, I made another follow up appointment with the neurologist. He reluctantly agreed to see us although he was certain that things remained unchanged.

Upon our arrival he conducted the now familiar battery of neurological tests. I anxiously awaited his assessment, my palms sweating. To everyone's astonishment, especially that of the doctor, Mikhaela had made an almost complete recovery.

She was still struggling a bit with her vision and fatigue, but that resolved over the next few months. The doctor was so amazed he asked what we had done. I described the treatment and the diet and referred him to the treating physician. It is now standard of care to use hyperbaric therapy for a variety of medical conditions.

Of course, Lake Norman continued to be our refuge and it was especially true of that challenging summer.

19

MIKHAELA

Have you ever been so sick that you are scared to go to sleep because you are unsure if you will wake up the next day? I have.

Most of my life I have only known physical weakness. Constantly in and out of hospitals, always missing school. On one occasion I returned from school after a long absence a classmate approached me and said,

"You are here? We thought you had died."

Unsure of how to respond, the first thought that came to my mind was that if they really did think I had died, no one sent any cards! I chose to keep silent.

When you are that sick you stop caring about the usual things. You stop being sad you can't go out of the house because you are just too tired. Finding joy in simple things like having enough energy to decorate the door of your bedroom. Time starts blending together. When you feel well again, you wonder how long it will last. Knowing that your family is worried about you but won't tell you.

Hospitals and illness were a very large part of my childhood. I was never a healthy child. In addition to having autism, I spent many weeks in the hospital for one reason or another due to comorbid conditions. I also always seemed to get the rarest types of illnesses, including cerebella ataxia in the eighth grade. During this time, I didn't know if I would ever be able to dress myself on my own or walk again much less have an active lifestyle. Sports and activeness were mostly inaccessible to me throughout childhood even if I wanted to participate. The inability to regulate body temperature meant I overheated easily and had to skip field days. Lack of coordination and depth perception made most sports extremely difficult. I constantly was falling off the weight charts. Certain girls at school accused me of being anorexic. I never would have imagined that a fit lifestyle would be in my future or that I would ever be physically strong. I had accepted my weak body.

In my adult life I am blessed beyond measure. I am the healthiest I have ever been and am rarely hospitalized. I am a yoga instructor!

At first, I thought,

How can the girl who walks into walls ever be coordinated enough to participate in yoga?

But like everything else in my life, I tried.

Yoga ended up providing not only a way for me to build muscle for the first time in my life, it gave me a safe space to be my autistic self.

I went to a handstand workshop where we all flapped our hands to warm up our wrists, and it was one of the happiest moments for me. I have never been a room where everyone flapped their hands with me. It created such pure joy and excitement within.

In a tai chi class, we stood on our toes because it activates a pressure point and is said to help with long life.

It was in this moment I realized,

What I do naturally as an autistic person isn't actually unusual.

In a lot of ways, autism is a very natural way of being. I am toe walking because of these pressure points, which made me wonder what else do I do naturally that society says is abnormal. In this class, people were actually *trying* to learn to balance on their toes, which was a natural state for me before I learned to repress it. I had been stimulating myself all along but didn't understand it.

As I became more active, my digestion became better, along with gravitational security and the ability to regulate my breathing. I am able to get the weighted feeling I crave from sandbags. The body crashing I seek from different poses. I've always had trouble feeling connected to the earth, as if I could drift away at any moment.

Now I have my health. It has become an integral coping skill for sensory overload and social anxiety. It has given me friends, along with a way to socialize (with a beginning and an end time so I am not overcome by an undefined amount of social time, allowing me to better prepare. Yoga classes, hiking, and other activities have all been perfect for this.

These types of activities are also great for me because they are not team centered; rather it is more of an individual based sport. When considering sports for autistic children things like swim teams, tennis, or the position of goalie are ideal. It allows for individual participation in a team setting.

I am grateful I was able to experience sickness early in life because it taught me how to be positive and how to adjust my routines no matter the situation. I do not take my mobility for granted.

The feeling of getting strong, especially for someone like me who has always only ever known physical weakness, is an indescribable experience. It provides me with confidence and joy.

20

MARY LYNN

F all brought a new school year as Mikhaela entered ninth grade. Although this was the official start to high school academically, it was the last year of junior high school in the grade configuration grouping. In her school, junior high included seventh, eighth, and ninth grades. This worked out especially well as it afforded her an extra year to develop socially before going onto high school with older, more mature students. Mikhaela relished the new academic challenges. Of course, math and linear thinking continued to be arduous. Literal thinking dominated as always. Reading, research, and writing were then and continue to be her strengths.

Ninth grade brought another lesson. I became ill and required surgery. I was weak and mostly bedridden for six weeks. It was a frightening time for all of us, and yet again, it was my mother who rose to the occasion. She took the children to and from school, prepared meals, did laundry, and of course, helped with homework. By this time, we had become a well-oiled machine. Although the nagging question is in the back of every parent's mind about what would happen if they could no longer care for their children, I think it is especially so for parents of children with disabilities. We all felt it keenly during this time, what would happen after I was gone?

Mikhaela was certainly dependent on me in ways that were not easily transferable. I renewed my determination to push her as much as possible toward independence.

This was also the time we decided to discontinue medication. The side effects were outweighing the benefit. It took about three weeks to taper completely off. I sent a memo to the faculty addressing symptoms they might observe during this period such as toe walking, rocking, hand flapping, or increased anxiety. Although we saw a slight increase in these behaviors, Mikhaela was able to quickly bring them back under control. Faith saw us through.

The end of ninth grade was bittersweet. We would be leaving Summit School...the place that had taken a chance on a struggling second grader, and had not only seen her through some daunting times, but had taught her to lead with her strengths and propelled her further than any thought possible. The faculty had used every teachable moment available. And they did it seemingly effortlessly, naturally, as they do for every student. I was now faced with the formidable task of finding a good fit for high school.

I began this process by making a list of the most important things needed for an educational setting. These included small class size, a fair amount of structure, academic challenge, compassion, and of course, a great theatre program!

The local choices included the public high school, which was entirely too large, an independent school, a catholic school, or home schooling. The independent school was cost prohibitive and separated students according to their ability or lack thereof. I didn't feel home schooling was a good option because we needed the daily practice with social sillies. I took Mikhaela to tour the Catholic High School. She immediately fell in love with it. They offered a wide range of classes including Advanced Placement, and it was steeped in structure and predictability.

We attended the school's spring production of, "Thoroughly Modern Millie." It was superb! They also had a program called Harvard Model Congress. Students were given an issue and travelled to Boston to compete in debate. Mikhaela was thrilled! It also offered the added benefit of a spiritual component. In keeping with my resolve to push her toward independence, I no longer volunteered to chaperone. I did, however, stay active behind the scenes. I kept in contact with teachers but only on conference day. I also became a board member, which enabled me to give back.

Mikhaela insisted on entering this school known only by her name and not by a diagnosis. Onward and upward!

Just because she was not identifying as autistic at school did not mean that the challenges she faced magically went away. I began to notice how exhausted she was after school. Masking her symptoms – and compensating – left her bone-tired.

But she powered through.

21

MIKHAELA

People with autism often are said to have no empathy. I disagree. It's the opposite. We feel too much because we feel everything all at once. As a result, we cannot distinguish which feeling should be placed in each situation. Because I feel and experience so much at the same time, I am not at all sure what emotion to attach to a given situation. With regular empathy, people draw on basic emotions they know and have felt. They intuitively are aware of which one they would feel in the other person's situation even if they have never been in it. They can empathize, which they do by using these basic emotions of anger, sadness, and happiness and applying it to the person's circumstances.

I do not know which basic emotion would be appropriate for a specific scenario. My emotions are as unpredictable and as intense as my sensory overload.

For example, have you ever witnessed a great historical tragedy so big that you don't even begin to know how to feel or process it such as a major tragic news story? That is how I feel with every unfamiliar emotional scenario. It's not that I cannot understand the emotions…it's that I experience *so many emotions* that I have no idea which particular one the person in front of me is feeling. In reality, a typical brain is likely only experiencing one basic emotion per situation. For me, I have no way of knowing which feeling is appropriate since my own emotional range is unpredictable, resulting in an emotional flood. I then internally filter through the onslaught and assign what I believe to be the appropriate reaction to the situation.

As an example, I remember in kindergarten I used to stick my tongue out at people to see what emotion it would illicit. Does my action cause anger? Happiness? I had no idea until I tried it…because I cannot know intuitively since I am unable to read nonverbal behaviors. Someone sticking out her tongue at me would cause *no emotional response* if done to me. It is meaningless because I do not assign the same values you do to nonverbal cues and behavior. So while people assume I am not empathizing, in fact I am. I just would personally not be feeling a reaction because I don't know the social value a nonverbal response may cause for someone.

You cannot properly empathize when the emotions you experience in each situation are not uniform. Our emotional experience is different, and therefore we have to learn why certain non-verbal things could be upsetting. It is not the least bit upsetting to me.

I reject the theory that we cannot empathize. We empathize on a different plane.

I am here, I am capable, and I care about people. I just show it in different ways.

22

MARY LYNN

Tenth grade brought another rite of passage and gateway to independence, driving. Just the year before, during the cerebellar ataxia crisis, it seemed as though driving would be out of the question due to the damage to her vision. With that now resolved, it was on to driving school.

Once again, I committed to allowing her the chance to try first and accommodate if needed, a policy that served us well. This may have been the scariest letting go experience to date, but I reminded myself that it was nerve-racking for most parents. Mikhaela passed the written section with flying colors, as I knew she would. After all, it was about rules! Then she completed the portion with the driving instructor, and it was time for me to get in the car with her at the wheel. Words cannot do justice to the mixture of pride and fear I felt.

I could barely believe we were sitting in this place.

Every limitation and bleak prognosis, every

meeting with doctors, therapists and educators, and every trepidation swirled in my head like a tumultuous ocean threatening to overtake me.

As Mikhaela turned the key in the ignition, I took a deep breath, steadied myself, and said a prayer of safekeeping and gratitude. The girl who would not ever be able to tie her shoe was going to drive a car.

23

MIKHAELA

As if human social language weren't enough, I was now learning nonverbal language of the road. Driving is not an easy task. I can hear each car's tires on the road making it difficult to tell how close something is behind me, my lack of spatial relations makes parking and lane changes hard, and night driving is all but inaccessible because oncoming headlights and streetlights feel like looking directly into the blaring sun without sunglasses.

Driving causes anxiety for many people, but I can hear every tire on the road speeding by at the same volume as a passenger sitting beside me. I have to process visually and auditorily at fast rates. I have found that playing music while driving will create more focus as it drowns out other sounds. Driving alone is always much easier. It is challenging for me to speak to someone and drive at the same time.

Just as in real life, I take the slower way around.

I'm not made for the busy highway. Maybe that way is faster and more convenient, but I prefer the back slow-paced roads. My love of following the rules doesn't go well on highways where people so often enjoy speeding. Isn't it funny how the very social rules neurotypicals create are so quick to be broken by the people who think they are important?

I avoid driving at night because of my extraordinary sensitivity to light. I always scope out my destination beforehand. Using Google Maps, I ensure there is a nearby parking lot and I like to see an image of what the building looks like and what landmarks I can expect to see. I carpool whenever possible and arrive early to eliminate stress. My brain is not very spatial, and I depend on my car's back-up camera to help me. I failed my first driving test for not being able to back up in a straight line. I have never needed to use that skill, but I do use three-point turns regularly...my autistic mind is always getting lost. Directions, even with a GPS, are always a gamble.

24

MARY LYNN

High school brought with it challenges, successes, and failures as it does for all students. The theatre continued to be a source of joy and hard work. Mikhaela carried a demanding course load and defined her self worth by academic accomplishment. This could prove to be a dangerous path. I reminded her that comparison to others is not a helpful or healthy measure, and I tried to instill in her, and her sister Meleana, that they are children of God. They have value because of the life breathed into them and the gifts they inherently possess. The key, I tried to ingrain, is to work diligently to develop those talents and give back to the world. It seemed especially difficult in the high school and college years for Mikhaela to hold onto that. It seemed as though no matter how much success she experienced, she was often focused on the student who achieved more. When you are unsure of yourself in a world that is constantly changing, you look to others as a gauge. This is why acting came with such ease – and was such a blessing in Mikhaela's life.

In eleventh grade, Mikhaela had an opportunity to compete in a program called Harvard Model Congress. This played to her strengths. It required research (which she loved) followed by a debate. There was just one obstacle. The competition was in Boston. She would fly with her team and teacher, stay in a hotel, compete, and then fly home. Luckily one of her best friends from childhood was also selected. He would be her eyes, ears, and navigator through the sensory onslaught of airports and hotels. As always, we practiced and talked about all of the things she would likely encounter and the strategies that could be employed. Winning an award was overshadowed by the sheer exhaustion that lasted nearly a week. Mikhaela loves to travel and the lesson learned here was to take a buddy to help navigate. And, of course, it is always more fun to share your adventures!

Another hurdle presented itself in the junior year of high school, the SAT exam. Mikhaela definitely wanted to attend a four-year university. I had pulled her out of standardized testing in elementary school due to her inability to perform well and the anxiety the tests produced. Most autistic minds are very literal in nature and Mikhaela's mind is no different. She has always done well in the classroom but has had difficulty demonstrating her knowledge on standardized tests, especially multiple-choice questions. Essays provide a better snapshot of her knowledge. Math continued to be daunting and dismal. Mikhaela discovered after taking the test the first time that there were several issues. The large room filled with hundreds of students proved difficult from a sensory standpoint. Add to that, not being allowed to get up, nor bring in a water bottle, along with the onerous task of lining up the correct answers with those pesky little bubbles. If one is filled in incorrectly, it throws off every other answer. Mikhaela would sit for the test three times before finally achieving a score that would be considered at the universities to which she wanted to apply. The score was minimal, but at least Mikhaela would be able to get the application reviewed. She was accepted at two schools and chose to attend High Point University. The president of High Point University is an innovative thinker who encourages students to become extraordinary. HPU also provided a living situation where Mikhaela would have her own room, as every student did. The configuration was two to four bedrooms with one common sitting area and small kitchenette. She could close her door and retreat. It was a perfect fit!

A very wise teacher told me, during this time, that the goal is not to claw your way into the most prestigious school you can, but to find the perfect school that allows your child to develop her talents.

I recommend that all students apply early in the fall of their senior year, thus enabling one to hear about the admission decision earlier. It avoids not having a place to land when Spring arrives.

After all of this hard work and an excellent outcome, it was time to return to the lake.

The summer brought sweet refuge. Mikhaela, Meleana, and I basked in the unhurried pace, warm sunshine, lapping water, amazing sunsets, and fabulous food that defined our treasured time there. My mother, ever supportive, nurtured us. We read and laughed and watched movies. Life was good.

Senior year in high school was filled with another demanding academic schedule, drama productions, and the challenges of navigating friendships. Mikhaela still had extreme difficulty with humor and sarcasm which are, of course, the trademarks of the high school social scene. These are areas that still challenge her today, and I often receive text messages from her asking for help deciphering dry humor and innuendo. Spring arrived. Mikhaela graduated from high school, and Meleana graduated from Summit School (9th grade). Again, a swirl of emotion engulfed me. It was certainly not lost on me how far we had all come. But I did not feel I could exhale yet.

Once again, Mikhaela was sailing into unchartered waters. There was no map. She would have to set her course as she travelled forward.

In what felt like the blink of an eye, it was time for Mikhaela to pack up and move to college. I worked hard to keep my emotions in check as most mothers do when their children are fledgling. We talked about strategies for successful college living. I encouraged Mikhaela to get plenty of alone time, noise-cancelling headphones, favorite food and water in the fridge and, of course, "Baa."

The university is about forty-five minutes from our home by car. It was far enough for Mikhaela to become more independent but close enough to access support when needed. At the end of the summer, once her schedule of classes was in hand, we made a trip to campus. We practiced navigating from the dorm to her classes. The dining hall and student store were added to the map.

Then moving-in day arrived. We loaded her car and a pickup and headed out. We joined the long line of cars on move-in day, and I felt as I did when I enrolled her in kindergarten, grammar school, and high school. And I was relieved that we were achieving another milestone. With each juncture came pride and joy in the accomplishment combined with apprehension and trepidation regarding Mikhaela's transition to the next step. I felt like I could not fully embrace the experience. My mother, her cup always running over, guided and supported me with faith and love.

After Mikhaela was settled into her college dorm, there was one last kiss on the top of her head and it was time for me to leave. As the car pulled away, the campus became smaller in the rearview mirror. I was overtaken by emotion. Yes, it was the letting go that tied me to other mothers and gave us commonality but unlike other parents, my concerns for the future were very different. I did not worry about drinking or not studying. I worried about other things: would Mikhaela get lost on campus, would the stressors of college and sensory overload cause her autistic symptoms to re-emerge, would she be able to make at least one friend, and what about dating? College presented a whole new world of social situations to navigate.

Mikhaela flourished in the new academic challenges. She settled on a major of political science with an eye on law school, a lofty goal. Her major required only one math class, and she set out to once again define herself in terms of scholarly achievement. As she learned in high school, this can be a dangerous path. I did not question her, and she continued to excel. She got a part-time job in the student survey research center, which played to her strengths. She was appointed to the Student Government as a prosecutor for honor code violations, which was an ideal position for somebody who loves rules. Friends were made through these activities. There were still daily text messages asking for help deciphering the social code, and I assisted as best I could.

During the summer months, Mikhaela took classes and lived at the lake.

I was at work when Mikhaela called. She was living at the lake with my mother.

"Baba says she is having a heart attack," she said.

I immediately switched to clinic mode burying my own emotional distress. I instructed her with short simple steps:

"Put the dog in the spare bedroom and close the door."

"Call 911."

"Stay on the phone until the EMTs arrive."

"Make sure to find out to which hospital Baba will be transported."

Mikhaela hung up with me and followed the directions exactly and flawlessly. After what seemed like an eternity, came another phone call.

"Can you speak to the EMT?" she asked.

I could overhear the dog barking behind the closed door. A voice came on the line and explained that my mother was indeed suffering a massive heart attack. She was being airlifted to the hospital in Winston-Salem, which was 45 minutes from the lake and 15 minutes from where I was working.

"She was breathing when she left, but I don't

know how she'll be doing when she arrives. She's in pretty rough shape."

I went straightaway to my longtime family friend's house, who was a retired surgeon and well connected. Luckily, he lived close by to my work. He calmed me and instructed me as to where to meet the helicopter. Of course, I was also concerned about my autistic daughter who was now alone at the lake.

There are many things I love about living in a small southern town: a cold RC Cola on a hot humid day, the sweet scent of magnolia, jasmine, and wisteria wafting through the air, and people saying hello when they pass. Faith is in action - and not just on Sunday. Random acts of kindness are not just the latest trend but have been a way of life for generations. In that spirit, a remarkable thing happened. The first responder, after packing my mom onto the helicopter, returned to the lake to check on the young autistic girl who was now alone. Amazing Grace.

My mother was rushed to surgery upon her arrival at the hospital. The doctors were able to save her life but the extensive damage to her heart was done. It would change our lives forever. And it was the little girl, who would never be able to tie her own shoes, who saved her grandmother. The lady who had given so selflessly of her time, her talents, and her treasures to give that little girl every fighting chance to succeed.

We spent that summer healing together at the lake, all of us. My mother was extremely fatigued and weak but determined to get stronger, her rose-colored glasses firmly affixed to the bridge of her nose. Just after the Fourth of July, as we were having a cup of tea, mom became quiet and pensive. I waited with her in the moment as she gathered her thoughts. Finally, she spoke.

"I've missed my chance to retire and live at the lake."

Ever my mother's daughter, I immediately developed an action plan. This had always been her dream. First the dream to live at the lake with my father was cruelly snatched from them when he developed and died of pancreatic cancer. Now it seemed that it might be permanently out of reach, taken by a failing heart. I saw to it that Mom remained at the lake from that moment forward. In fact, she never returned to Winston-Salem. We moved the best of 34 years of belongings to surround her with her favorite and most comforting memories.

This new arrangement gave Mikhaela, Meleana, and me the opportunity to give back to my mother just as she had given so much to us. Even as her health failed, she provided us with powerful lessons in grace and dignity.

Fall came. Mikhaela and Meleana returned to school, and I lived about an hour and a half from the lake. I spent two days a week at the lake, helping Mom with her shopping, housework, and therapy. She continued to be stable but never fully regained her strength.

Spring arrived, and brought with it a joy that we had fought so hard to achieve. Mikhaela graduated college. The impossible had become possible. Mikhaela graduated in three years, cum laude. She was featured as an extraordinary leader in her final year, and for the first time in her life, identified as autistic publicly. The local news did a feature story on her, and she slowly began to speak openly about her journey.

Meleana graduated from high school, making plans to attend Radford University. My mother, who has supported both the girls emotionally and financially, was too weak to attend either ceremony. It was her proudest moment. A greater unconditional love could never have been.

We all spent the summer at the lake. I commuted the 45 minutes to Winston-Salem to work and the girls helped tend to their grandmother when I was out of the house. Mikhaela had been accepted to law school. She would live in an apartment in Charlotte, NC, which was another huge step toward independence. Once again, anxiety reared its ugly head. We tackled the issues of independent living one at a time. We selected an apartment which was walking distance to the school in a safe neighborhood. It was more expensive than living commuting distance but left less chance of getting lost. It also eliminated the sensory overload of the train or having to find parking each day. There was the added benefit of walking. Exercise is a great strategy to combat stress. We carefully practiced the route to school and to the grocery store and to any other necessary destination.

The next hurdle was finances. During the college years, we had opened a bank account for Mikhaela that was linked to mine. I did the same for Meleana. We started with a monthly budget. They both did well with this. And it provided the extra security that if there were a mistake or special circumstance, I could transfer funds.

The first few months proved challenging. Academics were Mikhaela's refuge as always. Cautiously following the rules, success came as she transitioned to daily adult living. She paid the rent and bills on time. Learning to buy groceries and plan meals took a little more effort but was mastered within a few months. Mikhaela continued to grow throughout her law school career. She served on Moot Court and was elected president of the honor society. There was personal growth as well. She ventured out on small car trips to visit friends. First she traveled to different cities in North Carolina, and eventually out of state. We are all grateful for GPS.

The summer before her final year of law school, Mikhaela announced she wanted to travel to Lithuania on a study abroad program. I was sick with worry at this idea. If she were to become lost or sick, there would be no way for me to help her. She was determined, and so I stepped out in faith yet again. We put strategies into place. She would travel with a university group and have a travel buddy. She would contact me once daily, even if it was only a one-line text or email to let me know she was alright. I had an itinerary. I took a deep breath and dropped her off at the airport. It was a six-week program. As the days wore on, I found myself more at ease. She was so happy. She made side trips on the weekends to surrounding countries and her enthusiasm was positively contagious. Apprehension was replaced by excitement when she called. I loved hearing the joy in her voice as she relayed her adventures. She also visited Krakow, Poland from which my mother's family had immigrated. Of course, this thoroughly tickled Mikhaela's grandmother. The summer was filled with history and family stories.

Mikhaela finished law school, and sadly, my mother was again too weak to attend the ceremony. I did take her to the baccalaureate service the day before graduation but that proved to be difficult. We planned a lovely party at the lake where everyone was able to participate. It was a truly beautiful and happy day.

After graduation, Mikhaela returned to live at

the lake. She studied for the bar exam, though her heart wasn't in it. She was burned out academically and emotionally. The summer also brought profound loss. First, a friend of Mikhaela's from high school passed away from an unknown heart defect, followed by Meleana's childhood friend tragically committing suicide. It was a reminder of the fragility of life. Both passed in July as Mikhaela was sitting for the bar exam. After the exam, she took a contract job doing evidence review. The results of the test were released. She did not pass, and she was devastated.

The decision was made to skip the February bar exam and try again the following summer. My mother's health was deteriorating, and we all celebrated Christmas together.

Mikhaela was floundering. She was in a phase of life we all face at some point. Even though she had followed all of the rules, success was not coming easily. This is a very scary reality for an autistic mind. Living by the rules provides a sense of security. When life deviates, it is especially difficult to see how to change course. But there was a bigger purpose unknown to us at this time.

25

MIKHAELA

Being defined as a number is hard for anyone, but especially if you have a learning disability. For me, autism is a disability in many ways, but perhaps the most frustrating way is standardized testing. My IQ is completely skewed. While I test in the top percentiles on the verbal sections, my spatial and math IQs are grim. Because of the disparity, my high IQ is able to compensate for the part of my brain that tests at an extremely low level, evening me out to average intelligence. Meaning, an IQ scale is simply not an accurate predictor for my neurotype. However, this discrepancy becomes apparent anytime I need to think spatially, in patterns, or in numbers. How does this impact me? I cannot perform well on standardized tests. Standardized testing is all about patterns, something I will never be able to learn. Just as I will never be able to do jigsaw puzzles or think spatially.

Barriers were created for me based on being a number. Because my number has never reflected my capabilities. True, it accurately reflects the fact that I cannot think in patterns, but I already know that. What it fails to demonstrate is how I am able to compensate for that inability by playing to my strengths employing the verbal part of my brain.

To make matters worse, when I was in the eighth grade, I suffered brain damage. I contracted a virus, which then continued to attack my brain stem, causing cerebella ataxia. This impacted my spatial thinking even more. I saw everything on a slant as if it was leaning to the left, and my motor skills were severely impaired. Miraculously, I recovered, gaining all of my physical functions back after being home schooled for a year. However, some things never fully healed, including my spatial awareness.

My mind is the perfect storm to fail at standardized testing. None of my strengths are tested this way. Even when it includes subjects in which I excel, when it comes in the form of multiple-choice, I am unable to process the answer. I have been denied admission to schools I was more than qualified for based on standardized test results - despite having an outstanding GPA. I spent hours after school every day studying for the SAT, which I took three times just to get a score that would allow me to apply to college. Just as the SAT did not come easily, neither has my licensing exam.

I graduated from law school in 2016. In order to practice law, you must pass the bar exam.

This is a standardized test that tests every single area of the law. The pass rate is difficult even for those who are typically functioning. The first time I sat for the exam, I was an anxious mess. People would say things like "if someone doesn't pass the exam, it's because they didn't work hard enough, I don't know how someone could not take this seriously." These toxic comments were meant to make the bar studiers feel better about their own progress, but they were not aware that I knew there was a good chance I wouldn't pass because of the challenges of autism. Nothing was meant with ill intent, as many did not know about my disabilities, but this culture made it difficult for me to have confidence. I took this to mean that if I did not pass, I hadn't worked hard enough. So, I worked. I took a course that was not made for my learning style because that was how everyone else was learning, and I studied until I was burned out. Before this, I had never suffered burnout before. I was drained and could not learn the way I needed to. Additionally, tragedy struck the days I was taking the bar exam. My friend from high school passed away, and my sister's friend, who had grown up with us, died as well.

Needless to say, I was not successful. Not only that, I was the only one in my friend group who did not pass. My friends moved on with their legal careers, and I sank into a depression, feeling as my life was on hold. My number wasn't good enough. I was not good enough.

Eventually, things turned around for me. I finally found a job after spending over a year doing contract work that did not pay well. I fell in love with my new role, where I was using my legal knowledge and applying it, but not actually practicing so I did not have to be licensed. Despite my success, I wanted to try again. For my own fulfillment, I wanted to be esquire.

I took it a second time, now in a much better space. When I received the results, I almost laughed. I had missed the mark by one point. A strange thing happened. I felt a tremendous wave of accomplishment. True, I hadn't passed, but to come that close meant I had done the impossible. The girl who can't do puzzles or tie her shoes was only one point away from passing a brutal multiple-choice section. In that moment, I knew I had to try one more time.

They say that the third time is the charm. Team "3 and free." That's what I wanted to write. But that is not my story. I didn't get the inspirational ending this time. But I still got a happy ending.

Looking at the initial list and not seeing my name on the test takers that scored a UBE score high enough was incredibly frustrating. I felt I deserved it and that I'd worked twice as hard as anyone else to earn it.

I asked, "why couldn't I, just this once, experience success the same way as everyone else?" or "why do I always have to fight so hard?"

Here's my answer: because that would be a very dull story indeed. If I experienced success in the same way as everyone else, I wouldn't be who I am. I wouldn't have my wonderfully unique mind. Are there other autistic people that have passed, some even on the first try? Yes. Am I any less successful? No. Because this is my story. And my story is one where I find different versions of success. One where I create ways into the place I want to be when traditional doors repeatedly shut me out. I may fail, but I get up again. And because this hasn't come easily, I'm now better able to help others facing what are seemingly impossible obstacles.

However, this time, my story wasn't over. I opened my letter when it arrived, and my eyes filled with tears. My UBE score was high enough for a nearby state, even though I had again missed the magic number for my state. I could waive into another place. It wasn't the traditional way, but what about my life has been traditional?

I learned not to base my self worth on arbitrary standards the world assigns. It was only when I learned to let go and find happiness within myself that this success finally came to me. I had achieved what did not seem possible.

In the one and a half years I've been at my job, I have been promoted twice. I find such joy in the work I do, and I am using my degree. I have had more time to devote to writing my Edge of the Playground blog. Sometimes, we are pushed in directions that we did not initially envision, but it is where we are meant to be. It's impossible for us to judge whether we are successful or not because we don't know the whole story of our lives yet.

So, let's not define ourselves by numbers. Or by societal success. But by joy. And right now, I have so much joy! I have joy that I am able to score so well on a test I should have never been able to take in the first place. Joy I went to law school when I wasn't supposed to ever attend school at all. Joy that I have a job when I was told I would never work. Joy that I am able to write this and share my experiences.

Joy is the one thing that is everlasting. Don't ever allow the world to tell you that you aren't good enough because you never know when you may just achieve the impossible.

26

MARY LYNN

In the beginning of February, my mother had become gravely ill. I was so very thankful Mikhaela was living at the lake. We were working closely with hospice. By the middle of February, I stopped working and moved in with them. I watched, awe-inspired as my autistic daughter stepped into the role of caretaker. We worked side-by-side tending to her grandmother's needs. Meleana came home on the weekends. The lessons handed down for generations were well ingrained. Relatives visited one last time. We laughed. We cried. We prayed. On February 25, 2017, the woman who gave us strength, taught us faith by example, and always demonstrated grace under pressure passed quietly and peacefully.

27

MIKHAELA

What no one tells you about grief is how truly ugly and terrifying it is. You have nightmares, you see things, and I personally slept with the lights on for weeks. Grief is a trauma and it impacts everyone in ways they never anticipate. But grief did something else to me that I did not expect. It triggered the hard parts of autism. The disabling parts of autism.

For years now I have successfully managed the difficult parts of autism. I rarely have meltdowns and I can keep myself together in most situations. But after my grandmother passed certain things started creeping up again. Soon, it came to a point where I couldn't control them.

In the first weeks I was toe walking again. I was fisting again. I was agitated. I was stimming constantly, and not the happy safe kinds of stim like spinning. I usually have some type of urge to do these things. But I can always control them and wait until I am in a safe space. This was different.

I felt like I was 8 years old again, unable to control anything. It scared me.

My initial thought was fear. I have worked so hard to be able function in this world. And it wasn't fear because I am ashamed of who I am. It was the fear that I would keep backsliding until I could no longer even handle simple sensory input anymore. And that is scary. I did not at all enjoy the time in my childhood where every touch felt so intense that I burst into tears. Or the feeling I had of being unable to go out in public because the lights and sounds were too much. Not being able to keep meltdowns at bay and having no way to cope in the everyday world. This is over-stimulating world.

Although it is still a lot, I can now manually filter a lot of this overload and aversion to sensory input. It was slowly becoming apparent that this might no longer be true.

So why was this happening? I have thought a lot about it and the symptoms that reappeared were things that I do to comfort myself. The toe walking and spinning, even the flapping and fisting are all forms of re-centering for me. It is my way of expressing myself and handling my emotions. It was something familiar to my mind.

In a time of crisis our brains do what is comfortable to heal itself. To all those on the autism spectrum that may face a time of crisis such as grief or a traumatic event I want to reassure you.

If you find like I did that you cannot control things that you were once more easily able to, don't fight it. Let your mind heal. Allow your neurology to be itself and take the steps it needs to become whole again. And know that even people who are not autistic experience major change during grief. These are not setbacks. It is simply part of the process.

Eventually, I did regain control. I still have trouble when I am overtired or stressed but this is normal for me. I no longer feel that my mind is unable to handle even the small everyday tasks that I worked so hard to regulate.

It will get better. In the meantime, allow people around you to help you. And take comfort that at least for me, this was not something that eventually led to me not being able to handle grocery stores or other sensory intense situations like it used to be. I did not completely burn out, although I came close.

I encourage anyone going through something like this to reach out and join groups or communities. The more you face it and talk about it, the better you heal.

Autism and grief will now forever be a very interesting subject to me. I think our neurology certainly handles the process differently. Autism never goes away. It doesn't disappear after childhood, and there will always be times throughout the lives of an autistic person where burn out may occur from going through something like grief. When the pure exhaustion of masking is too much to handle along with whatever else we are currently going through.

We all heal differently. Be kind to yourself. And to those who are not autistic, support us. Perhaps if society was more accepting, I would not be as fearful when my mask began to drop. Teach us to love every part of ourselves, even the hard or disabling aspects of who we are. So that when these occurrences do happen, we don't feel quite as helpless.

Autism is often hard. It is very hard. But I would never trade it for a neurotypical brain because it is such an integral part of who I am. Once I learned to love all of myself, I was able to find the unique gifts and joy this life has to offer me.

After all, isn't that what we all hope to find?

28

MARY LYNN

The funeral came and went. Mikhaela wanted to go to the church to help plan Mom's service. Luckily, Catholicism is steeped in tradition, ritual, and scriptures. After everyone went home, I returned with Mikhaela to the lake and stayed two weeks. It was then time for me to return to my life as well.

I worried about Mikhaela staying at the lake alone, but she was insistent. She continued to be diligent in efforts to secure a better job. But she was vulnerable and alone. At the end of March, I had surgery to replace both hips. My recovery lasted six weeks. It was during this time that an older man preyed upon Mikhaela. He moved into the lake house, and she didn't know how to handle it. He was manipulative. He told her he loved her. She took him at his word. It was Meleana who came to the rescue, exposing him and his true history and nature after ten months of deception.

Mikhaela finally dug herself out of depression

and sprang into action. She developed a passion for yoga and even became a certified yoga instructor. Shortly after that, she landed a phenomenal job and decided to sit for the bar exam once again. She began the two-month process of studying, and I joined her on weekends. This time, she missed it by just one point. To my surprise, instead of being crushed, it just increased her resolve to try again. The Edge of The Playground blog was launched. Her fervor motivated me to finish telling the story I had started so many years before.

Mikhaela was and is finally embracing her true self. Isn't that our goal as we raise our children? The things that seemed so critical at the beginning faded in the big picture. She still can't do multiplication, but she can use a calculator. She still cannot recognize faces or read nonverbal cues, but she has learned strategies to compensate.

And let's face it, tying your shoes is overrated.

Epilogue

I am not superhuman. I am not a savant. I am just me. If you take inspiration from my story, then I am happy for that. At the end of the day, I am just like you. I am human.

There were so many times I wanted to give up. Times where I thought, just this once I wish I didn't have to fight for accommodations. Just this once I wish I could go somewhere and not worry about not being able to recognize the faces of people I'm looking for. Just this once I'd like to be able to filter out sensory stimulus. Just this once, I'd like to not have to fight to be in this world.

But I stand here on the other side now. I want so desperately to tell my childhood self that there does come a day where all of my hard work will pay off. A day when I am happy and when the slightest touch doesn't send pain throughout my body. If I had given up at any moment throughout this journey, I would have never been able to experience the success of all the work I put in. I would have robbed myself of the chance.

Sure, it would have been easier to stay in the closet lining up Polly Pockets forever. But I would have never traveled or made friends. I would not have found ways to make the sensory input less overwhelming. I would not have found true joy.

Every single one of us, no matter who we are, can find success. I do not mean that everyone's life will look like mine. No two people, regardless of autism, have lives that look the same, but all still have meaning and purpose. We are all valuable by the very fact we draw breath.

There is no way to ever know when all of the effort you put in will pay off or even what form it will take. But it does happen. Often it manifests in a way that you do not expect and could not imagine at the time. And though as an autistic person faith often eluded me growing up because of my logical and rational nature, now here I stand fully aware that faith is what protects me beyond the safety of the edge of the playground. I understand now that the ability to tie your shoes does not determine your success.

None of us know what our lives will look like, but there is one thing I do know.

Our lives will be filled with joy.

Even through the tears and failures, no matter our struggles, joy remains.